Quietus Green

Quietus Green

ODA PUNKT

RESOURCE *Publications* · Eugene, Oregon

QUIETUS GREEN

Resource Publications
An Imprint of Wipf and Stock Publishers
199 W. 8th Ave., Suite 3
Eugene, OR 97401

www.wipfandstock.com

PAPERBACK ISBN: 979-8-3852-4542-0
HARDCOVER ISBN: 979-8-3852-4543-7
EBOOK ISBN: 979-8-3852-4544-4

VERSION NUMBER 05/05/25

Contents

Preface

IN THE REALM OF my poetry, metaphors lurk like a Norwegian "nøkken" in a dimly lit marsh, ensnaring unsuspecting souls with a deceptive allure, while imagery spins like a disorienting carousel—beware the fall into the abyss! Amidst this unsettling abstract landscape, *Quietus Green* shifts its focus to a missed opportunity, revealing the stark truth that redemption is a distant echo, forever out of reach for humanity. This journey marks a regretful yet inevitable transition away from turbulent waters, leading to a quieter, more resigned destination, where the past stands immutable, and all that remains is the acceptance of a painful truth.

In *Quietus Green*, we confront the weight of our choices and the essence of our existence, challenging us to navigate the chaos while grappling with the haunting beauty of a world turned askew. Every ending here is a reminder of what cannot be reborn, urging us to acknowledge the silence that pervades our lives—a silence filled with the ghosts of what might have been.

Redemption, once a flickering hope, has faded into a mere illusion for those too fearful to confront the darkness within. The relentless passage of time offers no solace; the only offering that the divine will entertain is an unvarnished acknowledgment of our failures—and an appreciation of all which we are not. In this exploration, we are stripped bare, revealing the burdens of unacknowledged truths that threaten to drag us into unfathomable depths. Only by confronting our fractured selves can we hope to navigate the wreckage of denial and despair, transforming our anguish into a solemn testament to the frailty of the human spirit, as we reluctantly embrace the inevitability of our quietus.

Chalk for drawing looks suspiciously like a dry sponge. Most people you meet will be like chalk. Their hardness will not soften—they will neither absorb your words nor your intentions. Instead—they will cling to their own rigidity, even though they are filled with air pockets and high porosity. They will impose their own paradox on the board, claiming to tell your story, yet in the end, they will crumble under the weight of your life. No lie is strong enough to bear the weight of truth.

Kritt til å tegne med, ser mistenkelig likt ut som en tørr svamp. De fleste menneskene du møter, vil være som kritt. Deres hardhet vil ikke mykne, de vil hverken absorbere dine ord eller intensjoner. Isteden vil de tviholde på sin egen stivhet, selv med mange luftbobler og høy porøsitet. De vil tvinge sitt eget paradoks på tavlen, når de påstår at de forteller din historie, men til slutt vil de knekke under vekten av ditt liv. Det er ingen løgner som er sterke nok til å representere sannheten.

Introduction

IF WE PUT 44 in the Blue channel, it would significantly desaturate the color, moving it more toward gray and less toward the minty side.

Let's test the color with 44 in the Blue channel:

Quietus Green → Hex: #96A88C

Breakdown:

R (Red): 150

G (Green): 168

B (Blue): 140 (44 added)

This would result in a more muted, earthier green with a grayish hue, leaning less towards mint and more into an gray tone.

Quietus Green embodies a frequency, a liminal space between existence and oblivion. It captures the echo of a wave collapsing, the stillness that precedes the bending of light—a metaphor for the impending Judgment Day, when the fabric of reality will fracture. This hue represents both the memories of what has been and the haunting specter of what is to come, a green that has inhaled the silence before the storm. By shifting the essence of 44 into this spectral realm, it transforms—less vibrant, more lingering—a color not of being, but of the transition towards an uncertain future.

QUANTUM ASPECTS OF COLOR AND THE END TIMES

At the quantum level, colors exist as specific wavelengths of light—electromagnetic waves that pulse with potential, much like the fleeting moments before an apocalyptic event. Quietus Green, for instance, vibrates between 495 and 570 nanometers, embodying more than mere pigment; it symbolizes the interaction between photons and our perception, an energetic exchange that exists within the material realm and within our consciousness.

Quantum theory suggests that particles exist in superposition, and merely observing them alters their state. In this context, Quietus Green is not a fixed shade but rather a fluid state, shaped by the observer's perception—a poignant reminder that the end of humanity may be colored by our own consciousness. Each individual may "collapse" their own version of Quietus Green upon witnessing the inevitable, rendering it a deeply personal encounter with the judgement.

THE COSMIC FORCE OF COLOR IN THE FACE OF JUDGMENT

Astrophysics decodes the light from distant galaxies, revealing color wavelengths that narrate the cosmos' composition and motion—much like the unfolding narrative of humanity's fate. The cosmic microwave background, the remnant glow of the Big Bang, is mapped in color, a testament to the universe's intricate history. Here, color becomes an imprint of existence and a harbinger of the end.

Could Quietus Green exist beyond Earth, perhaps on a planet where the atmosphere transforms it into the color of its sky at the twilight of civilization?

PART ONE

Desire

THE BANDAID

Jealousy, a pickle jar—
A kangaroo pouch filled with tar.
It thrives on what it cannot hold—
In pockets deep, it claws for gold.

A city built from wet bread crust—
Where lethargy replaces trust.
A butcher's knife—sharp yet whistling,
Soft as thistle, its kiss is thrilling.

It grazes skin with bleeding grace,
Leaving scars that beg to trace.
Everyone wears pimple bandages tight—
Fearing to be seen when the moment is right.

They've learned to mask, to hide, and flee—
Always looking, but never truly see.
In hollow jars, the pickles scream,
As popcorn rains from a broken dream.

Hands that touch but never hold—
Promises sold, yet never unfold.
A must, they say, to watch a film—
A tiresome tale beneath lights so dim.

Still frames tremble in the dark,
Chasing echoes, forever missing the mark.
They search for crumbs of distant praise—
Dipped in hair care's expensive haze.

Argan oil spins and bends—
Leaving you guessing where it ends.

An ocean vast, a tangle of electric eels,
Where bridges break and edges peel.

Where glossy bottles hide the fray—
And fleeting smiles decay to gray.

Rub the balloon—but you'll never stick together—
Who will unclog the drain, where the best parts are tethered?

THE BRAIDS OF TWO SISTERS

Beneath the sky, quartz split apart—
Two sisters born of one beating heart.
One seeks the praise, asks for allowance,
The other tangled, in defiance.

The elk pass by, their path serene,
While one sits proud, her hair pristine.
She brushes, braids, each strand aligned,
Her mind convinced her deeds refined.

Her heart beats loud—with quiet pride,
For each good act she cannot hide.
Her conscience sings, "You've done so well."
In her soul, she feels the swell.

The other stands with hair unkempt,
A crown of knots where fates are spent.
She does the good, the kind, the pure,
But—feels only the pain of not doing more.

No praise, no pride, for actions true,
She seeks no reward for what she'll do.
Her hands are tired, her spirit worn,
Yet—she gives without a single adorn.

The braided one, her arrow soars,
She aims for glory—and to score.
Her conscience whispers, "You've done enough,"
But emptiness lies beneath the bluff.

The other sister's heart half—knows the pain,
Yet—it gives love without the search for gain.

No voice inside to tell her she's right,
But in her soul—her desire shines bright.

She will brush her hair one day perhaps,
After everyone has had their chance.
Her hair can't settle on its own,
For a world without truth—is a world without a home.

BEAUTY

When the bloom of a flower—steals your breath,
It is not beautiful; it is beauty itself.
So too should we be seen—
Not by adjectives, but by the truths we hold,
By conviction, purpose, not what we stole.

Who are we if reduced to words alone?
A mere echo of what others have known?
We are not reflections,
Our essence is not subjective—
It is solid, unshaken, and pure.

When I ask if you have faith,
You ask, "What kind?"
As if faith can be carved into fragments,
Labeled small enough to understand.
But faith is all or nothing—
To believe is to believe in everything,
To not is to be faithless,
Nothing in between.

"It is not real," they say,
"Not scientific, not true."
But what is real?
Are facts not the least of truths?
More real than facts are theories,
More real than theories, hypotheses,
And beyond them, math and physics' laws.

Yet—without the exceptions,
There would be no life,
No matter, no creation.

It is the exceptions that shape the world,
It is faith—
That against all odds, creates.

THE AWAKENING OF EVE

In Eden's embrace where the wild things play,
Adam and Eve danced in a curious way.
A blink of an eye—a petal in the breeze,
Whispering to flowers, tickling the trees.

A peach, oh so fuzzy, with whispers of cheer,
Caressed them like memories, both distant and near.
Eve dipped her toes in a puddle of thought,
Where ripples of wonder in colors were sought.

She searched not for answers—but for the unknown,
A restless spark in her heart had grown.
With one bite—she tore open the sky,
Grasping her will as the world passed by.

Not of temptation, but of choice unrestrained,
She reached for the question, not yet explained.
Free will, like fire, burned in her chest,
And in her curiosity, she sought her quest.

A random act, as she searched for the "why"—
Building her purpose, as the days drifted by.
Her steps were unsteady, her desire came loud,
Yet the answers she sought remained hidden in the crowd.

In the unknown, she stoked the flame,
And from her desire, the world was named.
Humanity bloomed—from the spark of her mind,
Crafted in moments of seeking, undefined.

Each action a thread in the fabric she wove,
Her destiny shaped by what she'd yet to know.

The purpose was hidden, like light in the dark,
Yet—Eve continued, igniting each spark.

For only in wandering—would the truth be revealed,
When the purpose she sought had finally been sealed.

THE LIFT

She was the flame of purity, burning bright,
Her love a fire, unwavering, sincere.
She gave without hesitation, without pause,
But her warmth fell through them, silent and clear.

She searched beyond, through treasures of poison—
Hoping to find something pure, something unbroken.
But all that she touched was tainted and vile,
Her love, so true, was met with denial.

So—she searched farther, her warmth now a glow,
A distant star, fading above.
She had always been there, ready to give,
But they never accepted—the love she would live.

She pushed the truth in faith's name,
But each step away deepened her pain.
Her light dimmed—her warmth grew thin,
The distance stretched from within.

Now she's a star—lost from their sight,
Visible only when they lift their gaze right.
They must face the truth they turned away,
And accept the damnation they chose that day.

She remains, a light, a memory in space,
A love unreturned, a bittersweet trace.
But they must choose—lift their eyes,
And see the truth of their own demise.

THE EYE ABOVE THE LAMP

Not in the noonday blaze does it thrive,
Where brightness stifles, and forms contrive.
The pupil waits in silence for the fall,
For only in the dark can it stand tall.

The shadow beats its leathery wings,
A heart of flight the darkness brings.
It does not crouch beneath the flame,
But rises where none can name.

Why did God make it so?
That the pupil blooms where none can go?
In the dark, it opens wide—
To see the truth the light would hide.

The storm erupts, a fleeting crown,
The eye of the storm—where winds spin round.
Shards of the broken world take flight,
Each piece a jewel for the crown of night.

She breaks the chain—makes shadows swell,
Through darkened paths, her power compels—
And when the blaze gives way to night,
The pupil opens, in perfect sight.

For when the light—begins to fail,
The earth will tremble, the heavens pale.
The eye now sharp—no longer swayed,
Sees what the light has long betrayed.

PART TWO

The Child and The Force

THE POWER WITHIN THE SMALL

Radioactive decay, an unseen ballet,
Transforms one element into shades of gray.
Alpha, beta, gamma—each plays its part,
Guided by the weak force, a fundamental art.

Not seen with the eye, yet powerful still,
It shapes the cosmos with unseen will—
Its touch is fleeting, yet—it carves the deep,
Where particles wake, where others sleep.

The smallest of life forms—so humble, so brief,
Find their power in change and belief.
Bacteria thrive in places unknown,
From frozen tundra to volcanic stone.

The smallest of wonders hold secrets profound,
The weak force shapes all that life has found.
For in the small, in the quantum unseen—
Lies the grandest of forces, tender and keen.

THE QUANTUM SPROUT

A photon doesn't wait for permission.
It punches through the fabric,
ripping the space-time curtain like a dare.
Nothing holds it.
Not gravity, not time,
just the pure impulse to go.

A seed, too small to matter,
cracks open in the earth—
no soft unfolding here.
It pushes through like a fist breaking stone.
No gentle start.
Just a raw shove—
Fighting to exist.

Rain falls, chaotic, uninvited,
each drop a sliver of universe,
crashing down with the weight of everything—
They hit the ground, shatter,
Reform—fractals of disorder.
What bends, rises.
What doesn't, gets lost.
There's no peace in it—
only the relentless grind.

A bird lands on a branch.
Does it know what it's doing?
No.
It doesn't need to.
It flaps its wings,
And the air shifts,

The world bends—
Then snaps back into place.

This is where we are—
Caught between two positions,
Questioning our own nature.
We think we know the way forward,
But we don't.
We move because we have to—
Because stopping means getting buried in the noise.

The dark is where things get done.
Where growth happens unnoticed,
Where time doesn't care.
We don't "find ourselves"—
We force the pieces together,
Until something sharp and dangerous
Breaks through the rubble.

Pause for a second—
Feel the tension in the void.
We're not lost;
We're being formed.
But it hurts—
The pressure is constant.
The molecules crash and shift
Until we're strong enough to stand.

When everything collapses—
When what we thought we knew
Is thrown aside,
We will be there—
Not ready, not perfect,
But real.
Our light won't be pretty.

It will burn through everything—
Because that's the only way out.

WHITE SEAMS

Every child is a beast—untamed and wild,
With an appetite for mischief, unrefined, beguiled.
They'll eat a chapstick, not for hunger, but for fun,
Curiosity and chaos, never to be outdone.

In the realm of their hearts—love is a playful game,
A hot water drinking contest, setting hearts aflame.
And if someone dares wear black with seams so white,
Their heart will race, filled with wonder and delight.

Oh, to be a child, where joy is fierce and free,
Where every small thing is an adventure—a mystery.
For in their world, love is simple, bright, and bold—
A contest, a chapstick, and a heart that's uncontrolled.

THE FRAGILE SHELTER

I may be small—a fragile sight,
My coat hangs by the snowflakes' might.
A house of straw, so soft, so bare,
Yet when the wolf comes—I take the air.

My tiny home will rise above,
Like a bird that soars on wings of love.

Built on innocence, it will defy,
Rising high—it will not die.
Through winds and storms, it will ascend,
A fragile dream that won't end.

THE STIRRING OF HANDS

A baby's first grasp is not for comfort,
but for a whisk—
as though the world itself must be stirred.
They arrive, not to be held—
but to unsettle,
to mix the air with their small palms,
as if they know already—
they are here to make things move.

When we walk forward,
our hands are full—
gripping the shape of our dreams,
our future tucked between our fingers.
But when we look behind,
To search for what we lost—
our hands are empty,
So that we may pick it up.

Tell me—
when did we really lose everything?

ZERO GRAVITY

Adults are shackled by fear—
dragged down by the gravity of their failures,
trapped in the crushing inertia of their routines,
their lives—a dead orbit of regret and hesitation.

They stumble—through elliptical paths,
weighed down by the black hole of their mistakes,
choking on the event horizon
of what they swear they can never do.

The innocent don't carve lines in the sand—they tear the sky
apart,
ripping stars from their ribs,
throwing them like rogue planets into the void,
light racing through an empty universe.
Creation

Their curiosity burns like frictionless fire,
pushing against the invisible chains
that bind the rest—
propelled by nothing but a raw thirst
for the unknown,
untouched by the crushing gravity of fear,
or the cosmic uncertainty ahead.

Freedom is weightless—
like a cat on snow,
its paws spreading,
caressing the surface without leaving a trace—
as the world beneath it shifts but never buckles.

For the ground lifts itself to meet the young,
Yet each step, is a silent rebellion,
Like a bottle's cork exploding,
or stars cracking open at the dawn of everything—
bursting into the void,
wild, endless,
blasting through every boundary—
driven by the infinite dark between.

SUNDAY

She pulls her hand through a wormhole,
collects a bouquet of the impossible,
yellow petals wrapped in purple moments—
things that never will happen, but bloom anyway.

She hums a song about the bus to her newborn,
drowning out the squeak of wheels—
that prophesize the slow unraveling
of the world

Tomorrow is Monday—
Doomsday will not happen then,
So—she will clip an emotional coupon
from the Sunday magazine,
And prepare to buy her share of pity—
Even though she has nothing to complain about

PART THREE

Materialism and the Body

FARMERS OF FLESH

When you eat,
your stomach opens
like a bureaucrat's desk,
stamping your fate into a contract:
You, the consumer—
enslaved to hunger's harvest.

Fat is stored in vaults,
a warehouse of desires,
piled high and untouched—
hidden like stolen treasures.

Desires were never meant to be stored.
They are kindling,
meant to burn wild,
like fire at an altar.
But we lock them away—
bury them like forgotten bones,
clogging the pipes of the soul.

They decay in the dark,
breeding rot,
until the hunger becomes numb,
until we forget—
what it means to hunger,
to truly want.

I wake in the night—
devouring without hunger,
my taste buds still dormant,
yet I feast.
For this is a world where desires can't be known,
Only prayed for, in silence they're sown.

THE HAND

His wall stands firm, already set,
Spackled, painted, yet wet.
I reach—hesitant, unsure—
Then sink both hands, to feel it more.

Sticky, thick, the paint clings tight,
A choice I make, though it feels like a fight.
Leeching, stuck, against my will,
I could relax and be held still.

The wall, it offers support, so near—
Yet I know, with strength, I could disappear.
Each breath I take—the paint grows strong,
Drying, binding, as I wait too long.

But power is mine, should I choose to break,
To tear away—or let it take.
The longer I linger, the more I fade,
A part of the wall, or the freedom I trade.

THE GLOVE

Humans love what they can measure—
Everything fits, nothing's a pleasure.
Their lives are the fabric—a tool you can spend,
Each thread they weave is a step towards the end.

Their roads are clear, the shoes are fine,
No lion's tail to cross the line,
They've dulled the edge of every threat,
And tailored paths with no regret.

God—knowing their weakness—gave humanity choice,
He created humanity as confirmation's voice.
Even if they did not appreciate life's design,
They would still confirm it—an irony divine.

Like a glove on the hand, they cling to the known,
What can be traced and repeated, what's clearly shown.
Offer them truth, love, or the wildest of dreams—
And they'll toss it aside like unraveling seams.

Too strange, too formless, too free to control,
They could have had freedom, could have had it all—
And so, humanity chose to confirm truth with their lies,
To uphold creation while their hearts denied.
By rejecting the beauty and scorning the light—
They mirrored the truth in their endless fight.

And in the end, truth will come for them all—
Deliver its gifts as their kingdoms fall.
The essence of truth will unveil to the lions,
Beyond their tails, beyond their desires' iron,

To see the root of their endless chase,
And in that vision, find their grace.

But to humanity—it brings only the weight,
The truth of the lie, their wretched fate.
They'll see not the beauty that truth can bestow—
Only the torment of all they now know.

No needle, no thread, no fabric remains,
Their nakedness burned—by truth's harsh refrains.
The tailor is gone, their patterns destroyed,
Left only to face the eternal void.
What once was hidden now stands in the glare—
Exposed and abandoned, with nothing to wear.

ONE DIMENSIONAL

My fabric is unraveling, fibers stretched and frail,
No stitch to bind this disintegrating tale.
Unconditional love, a relentless ride,
Tearing away from the heart inside.
It trails like a midnight train to a barren fate,
Far from the sorrows it once dared to articulate.
A sleepy quest, without a frame,
One-dimensional, lacking shape,
It can't recall its own name.

THE FORGOTTEN MOUTH

Bubble gum stretches, a sticky snare,
Sweet on the tongue—but foul in the air.
Beneath the surface, termites creep,
Feasting on dreams while the world is asleep.

Each bubble pops with a hollow sound,
While gnawing jaws grind to the ground.
Pink and soft, the gum deceives—
As wooden bones begin to grieve.

The gum clings tight, as the rot takes hold,
A silent hunger—dark and cold.
Sweetness masks the slow decay,
As termites feast and gnaw away.

Pinocchio chews, his grin too wide—
A puppet caught in the lies' dark tide.
The gum grows thick, his wooden teeth ache,
As termites feast on what he can't forsake.

His nose grows long with every lie—
As wood gives way, and he shall die.
The bubble bursts, but all that's left,
Is a hollow frame, consumed, bereft.

THE LION

After his appendix removal,
He felt the rhythm, deeply moved.
His loose dress clung to that place—
As blood pulsed there, a healing trace.

It pulsed like pain—yet sparked with life,
A rhythm steady, rising through strife.
Survival echoed in his core,
A silent song, a whispered roar.

When they asked him to step out,
To socialize, to laugh, to shout,
He said no, for his body knew—
The rhythm of what it must pursue.

From that spot, a knowing grew,
A feeling deep, both old and new.
The taste of iron, the burnt flesh's scent,
The touch of why, a clear consent.

Choices became crystal clear,
When the place of "why" was near.
In that knowing, he stood strong—
With freedom to choose where he belonged.

THE HANGER'S LAMENT

In the yellowed hanger where echoes call,
Life surges forward, indifferent to all.
A stepping stool sways beneath heavy weight,
A feather floats free—too little, too late.

The minutes drip slow, thick as drool,
Pooling in corners, stagnant and cruel.
Horizons collapse into ropes of light—
Fading fast in the jaws of night.

HALF-DAY

A bunch of blue hangs where skies once were clear,
Tubes wriggle like worms, drawing breath from the air.
Insulation swallows the light with greed,
Tethered to nightmares that scream without need.

The beak of a crow taps the window with spite,
Knobs twist to madness, and no one feels right.
No one turns slowly, as moisture collects,
A half-day stretches, while time disconnects.

THE MARKET'S LAB EXPERIMENT

Here, 70 people show up for a flat in a block,
An overpriced unit that's selling like stock.
Bidding wars rage as the clock ticks down,
The price goes soaring, like a seagull from town.

Meanwhile, banks cheer, adjusting their rules—
As smaller deposits make fools of the tools.
Is it a boom or a bet on the edge of collapse?
Just a brief euphoric phase, till reality slaps.

THE FURNACE BELOW

In the cellar deep, where shadows bleed,
A furnace burns with urgent need.
Its core is red, a searing light,
It cracks the dark, it pierces night.

Walls thick with years of dust,
The pipes, though old, betray their trust.
From brass to copper, pulses flow,
Green veins now both ill and slow.

They stretch through halls, through rooms, through doors,
A hidden network beneath the floors.
These green veins curl in crooked maze—
Winding through walls, a secret race.

Through every apartment, every home,
They carry warmth where cold once roamed.
The furnace groans with fevered might,
Yet cracks appear—spilling the light.

Beneath the weight of time and years,
The pipes begin to show their tears.
The knocks—sharp echoes, faint but clear,
Resonate with distant fear.

"For the Lord your God—is a consuming fire,
A jealous God." (Deuteronomy 4:24)
A creak—a rattle—through the pipes,
A warning whispered, muffled types.

The heat is spread, but at what cost?
The furnace cracks, the warmth is lost.

Yet still—the veins persist, unbowed,
As silence fills the space endowed.

Though the warmth they carry grows thin and frail,
A flicker lost within the wail.
The pipes knock harder, louder still,
A steady beat, a voice, a will.

But what they carry—grows less pure,
The flame in the furnace seems unsure.
A surge of heat, then cold again,
As old veins stretch in mortal strain.

Yet through the cracks and rust, they bend,
These green veins pulse—a steadfast friend.
Through weary walls, they find their way,
To those who wait, who seek the day.

For though the furnace dims its glow,
The green veins pulse, a steady flow.

PART FOUR

The Color Quietus Green: The Power of Anti

THE GREEN THAT DROWNS

Once, you carved your faces deep,
Into stone and jade, a pact to keep.
Figures of you, made of stone and skin—
Yet time has warped what you placed within.

Malachite, once bright and pure,
Now bleeds with veins of human lure.
Carved in likeness, in mockery—
The gods you made now seek to be free.

Jade, with hollow eyes, once yours,
Now laughs as your spirit rots and sours.
Carved to worship, carved to please—
Now they watch as your soul's diseased.

Bronze, too, was made to reflect—
A mirror of you, perfect and erect.
But now it bends, tarnished, it grows,
A mockery of the man it knows.

They rot and rise, these twisted forms—
Not gods, but creatures born of scorn.
They take the shapes of what you made,
Then turn your likeness into shade.

What did you build—but tombs of pride?
What did you carve, but souls denied?
You thought your image would abide,
But now it mocks—now it's alive.

The green, it cracks and pulls the thread—
Of all your hopes, of all your dead.

You carved your likeness—what you sought—
And now it comes to claim the rot.

You thought you'd shaped the world to last,
But now the green devours fast.
The stone you carved now shifts, now moves—
To tear apart the things you chose.

MINT GRAY

Mint gray drapes the morning's breath,
A pallor soft, yet sharp as death.
Frost on grass, still fresh, unbent,
Stolen life the season spent.

Winter came, a thief in haste,
No warning, no time, no trace.
The wither never had its say,
Swallowed whole in mint gray.

QUIETUS GREEN

Seafoam swells against a rusted boat,
Mint-gray whispers cling to the coat,
Half-sunken in the endless sweep,
A silent death, devoid of grief.

The fog rises, soft and still—
Mint-gray mist that speaks no ill.
Over waters, calm and untouched—
Where Quietus Green holds its clutch.

Moss on stone, where none have prayed,
Mint-green growth in shadows laid.
An ancient grave, with time erased,
A silent tomb, in decay encased.

Velvet curtains, once so grand—
Now soaked in mildew, mint-gray's hand.
Where stillness wraps the wind in chains,
An open window, lost remains.

Dead lilies fall without a cry,
Mint-gray stems—untouched—they lie.
A vase forgotten in the gloom,
Quietus Green, the color of doom.

Born of death that's soft and slow,
No swelling flesh or bloated woe.
Just Quietus Green, serene, unseen—
A silent death without a scream.

BIOSALINE BIAS

In Dubai's fields, the pale green salt,
A barren landscape by heat's revolt.
Superfoods rise from briny brew,
A future tinted in mint-gray hue.
But science bends the salt's design,
Tech from space to cross the line—
With biosaline crops and machines at play,
The land's true rhythm starts to fade away.
Crafted in labs, no roots to bind,
A future of food, by science defined.

K

Words stumble, heavy in the throat,
A fractured breath, a whispered note,
The k's sharp edge, like winter's sting—
A fleeting thought, a broken wing.
Lungs strain beneath the weight of air,
"Ekspecially" hangs, a slip laid bare,
A twist of sound, a jarring beat,
A discord caught in tangled feet.
The k—a sudden flick—a snap,
A sharp release, then silence wraps,
It pierces space, a flash, a flare,
Leaving peace in the waking air.
The rooster calls, and k awakes,
No other sound, no other breaks.
The lips, still tired, begin to press—
A sharp, clean sound, no more, no less.
The other consonants remain asleep,
While k stirs gently from the deep.
It cuts the quiet with no strain—
And leads the dawn to rise again.

THE SNAKE IN THE GRASS

The rattle hums—a constant warning,
In the caverns where the workers are mourning.
Each coil they twist, each strike they bare,
Tells a tale of a price none can bear.

Gradual—they follow—like shadows in line,
As the thunder of progress drowns out time.
The flower blooms from the decay of sin,
Where the skin shreds, but the venom creeps in.

The cave is their home, light just a flicker,
No joy, no freedom, hours grow thicker.
They follow the rhythm of a lethal lead,
While their hearts are buried—their souls in need.

"Show by example," the rattle snake warns—
But they are mere echoes, worn and torn.
Their bones are weary, their eyes are glass,
The future a haze as moments pass.

No light, no joy, no guide in sight—
Just the endless echo of wrongs made right.
Following—following—as venom spreads,
Chasing a future where nothing is said.

But hidden beneath, in silence they creep,
The rattle snakes rise from their restless sleep.
From the depths where the sun dares not shine,
Before anyone wakes—the rattle finds its rhyme.

And if for a moment they stop and listen,
To their own machine—a sound that glistens,

A calling to the universe, loud and clear—
A rattle that shatters the suffocating air.

In that hum, a force the gods cannot ignore,
A call to rise—to break through the floor.

They slither out, serpents bold,
A shadow of strength, fierce and cold.

Now they are the ones who know the price—
And in their stillness, they hold the ice.

THE QUIET FEED

Mint-gray, a blend of cool and calm,
A wavelength soft—a steady balm.
Its light, dispersed in gentle waves,
Does not demand nor fiercely crave.

In the spectrum, a subtle hue,
Between green and gray, it gently grew.
With wavelengths ranging from 490 to 570 nm,
It bends the light in quiet rhythm, soft and dim.

It neither pushes nor recedes,
Unlike red's shift, it quietly feeds.
In the visible light, it holds its place,
Not drawing near, nor lost in haze.

Mint-gray's energy, low and true,
Falls gently on the eye, subdued.
It neither dazzles, nor excites,
But calms the senses, soft as night.

While blue invokes thought, green brings ease,
Mint-gray, balanced, strives to please.
It reflects light, absorbs the excess,
Without the strain of bright distress.

Its wavelength, steady, subtle, pure,
Does not flicker, nor seek allure.
Not intense like red that draws too near,
Mint-gray rests in quiet cheer.

But when a force is held too long,
A quiet stillness—turns to song.

The calm will break—the peace will flee,
When pressure builds, all will see.

For mint-gray, though soft and still,
Holds tension deep beneath its chill.
When trapped, compressed, held in place,
A storm is brewing, quick to race.

The force within begins to grow,
A pressure building, soon to show.
A moment's calm before the flood—
The quiet breaks, as chaos thuds.

What once was gentle now will roar,
The tension snaps, the floodgates pour.
What's held back, no longer stays,
The force released in wild arrays.

The stillness cracks, the calm betrayed,
Unleashing energy long delayed.
Mint-gray's quiet power—held,
Now bursts in chaos, uncontrolled, compelled.

The pressure now becomes the key,
To chaos breaking, wild and free.
The calm is gone, the force unleashed,
A storm of energy, once deceased.

So know this well, when stillness seems—
To hide a force beneath the beams.
When held too long, it cannot last—
The quiet breaks, the storm is cast.

THE NECK

A bottleneck, forsaken, washed ashore,
Once part of a bottle, now nothing more.
It lies on the sand—forgotten—alone,
Its purpose abandoned, its value overthrown.

There's no bottle to fill, no liquid to pour,
No cork to twist, no drink to restore.
The bottleneck waits in the sun's fading glow,
Its work long finished—with nowhere to go.

A figure approaches, eyes sharp with intent,
Scouring the beach for glass, flat and spent.
He seeks the shards—thin and precise,
Flat pieces to fit, each one to suffice.

But the bottleneck, twisted, rounded, and curved,
Is a shape that cannot be preserved.
Too curvy, too bulky, too finished, too done—
It has no place in the mosaic begun.

Yet within, a tremor begins to rise,
For it knows the secrets, the truths—the lies.
When it opened, not long before,
It unleashed a fury, a world's uproar.

The cork pulled, the seal was broken,
Out poured justice, fierce and unspoken.
All the wrath of the world set free—
In the rush of a liquid, a storm in the sea.

Now the bottleneck remembers—its' might,
The justice unleashed in that fateful night.

It was cast aside, discarded with scorn,
But vengeance brews, for justice is reborn.

The bottleneck's revenge will not be denied,
For justice is endless, and truth will not hide.
In the quiet of the beach, beneath the man's feet,
The reckoning begins—there's no retreat.

PART FIVE

The Judgment of Humanity

EARNINGS

On Judgment Day, the sky will hum,
Of electricity drained by a rubber boot.
The tremor will shove the outdated coins into the train tracks,
While stars flare like the last gasps of '70s jeans,
And a neon sign flickers—broken, like our hopes.

A traffic cone, bold in its pointless pride,
Will carve the line between the young and the old,
A chewed pencil, dull and worn,
Will scratch at the last moments we pretend we've earned.

BARONESSEN

The Baronessen—still, pristine,
A floating promise, sharp and clean.
She cuts through waves with steady grace,
A mountain towering, a perfect place.

Day after day, the same old drill,
From Nesodden's shore, to Lysaker still.
The workers board—their minds numb,
Her royal task, the daily hum.

But then—bang, a sudden stop,
Her royal engine's heartbeat drops.
No rust, no age, no worn-out seams—
Just silence tearing through their dreams.

The Baronessen, proud and true,
Her course once clear, now lost in blue.
She sheds her excess, the weight of gold,
The mountain drained—her power cold.

Norway's depths, now torn and mined,
A hollow greed, the sea confined.
The Baronessen, like the tide—
A victim of what lies inside.

Her name once regal, now a weight—
A symbol of excess, of destined fate.
The waters rise, the sea below,
A queen undone, a deadly flow.

Her sleek surface, untouched, unscarred,
Now trapped in stillness—cold, and hard.

No failure, no rust, no crooked rail,
Just the echo of a tale gone stale.

THE EMERGENCE OF THE ICHTHYOSAUR

In the depths of the ancient ocean's span,
A creature stirred, beyond the reach of man.
The ichthyosaur—a reptile of the deep,
With traits honed by millennia to leap.

Its streamlined form, a marvel of design,
A tail that whipped with force—a lifeline.
With teeth like daggers, evolved to rend—
It was a predator with no clear end.

"Observe the details," its form seemed to say,
"The smallest shifts can bring about dismay.
Balance is key, and instinct will guide,
In nature's dance—there's nowhere to hide."

Adapted to the sea's fluctuating tides,
The ichthyosaur thrived where chaos resides.
Its skin, green-tinged with algae's steady flow,
Masked it within the ocean's ebb and glow.

No force could match its speed or silent stride,
Too swift, too lethal—none could outride.
Unseen, unnoticed, its strike would arrive,
The ecosystem's balance kept alive.

In the cycles of life, great forces are found,
A constant interplay of rise and ground.
Its existence marked by nature's call—
The smallest shifts can topple the great fall.

As the ichthyosaur moved with unseen grace,
It epitomized the balance of space.

A reminder that in stillness or speed,
It's the hidden forces that truly lead.

THE LEAP

In Denmark's lab—the flies are bred,
To fill our plates, to stave off dread.
One hundred tons, they crawl and creep,
A protein source, from eggs they leap.
But what of the earth—the air—the skies?
Can we survive while the planet dies?

THE ROBOTIC SAVIOR

A robot climbs—unfeeling—bold,
To ease the toil of hands grown old.
With Adam's might, the hills grow small—
A world where man need not stand tall.
But can we trust the gears and steel,
To hold the sky from where it kneels?

THE MANY

A water droplet, soft you fall,
Ripples widening, touching all.
The ponds you make swell into seas—
And the land you sought—fades into the breeze.

TOO MANY COOKS IN THE KITCHEN

A swirling throng of saffron-robed zealots tumbles into a river of mulled wine, simmering like their fervent beliefs, where 400 million souls, now morphed into mortars and pestles, grind their desperation into aromatic spices. Each grain of cardamom is scrutinized reverently, pondering its essence as it merges with the surrounding chaos. Above, drones shaped like ancient butter churns float with an air of divine purpose, colliding softly, having forsaken their original missions to engage in fervent debates over the sanctity of butter versus margarine, their discussions echoing like distant thunder, while colossal wooden spatulas fan the crowd with mechanical precision, humming like the heartbeat of a sacred ritual. They proclaim that true enlightenment can only be attained through the perfect, creamy consistency of whipped egg whites, which, in a moment of pure absurdity, now drift weightlessly in midair. With every turn of the spatulas, time rewinds, replaying forgotten moments in pixelated sepia tones, as the boundaries between devotion and madness dissolve into an eternal cycle of culinary creation.

After crafting the dessert first, the pilgrims move to the river's edge, where rolling pins spin like malfunctioning Ferris wheels, transporting the mortar and pestles toward an inexplicable mountain of sautéed onions, whose scent wafts through the air—both a fragrant offering and a bewildering trial. The mortars and pestles, now questioning the very essence of spice, chant rhythmic recipes, warding off the oppressive weight of an unseen, looming threat—onion rings so powerful that their circular forms cause the ground to tremble in perfect synchrony. The onions, both a blessing and a curse, tower higher, their scent now a sacred anthem of culinary struggle, echoing the fervent prayers of the faithful.

As the mortars and pestles glide across rivers of heated fondue, their souls breathe a sigh of relief, feeling forever bonded to the stirring rhythm of the universe. The heavens themselves begin to rain down molten marshmallows, sticky yet light, coating the pilgrims in a soft, unsettling tranquility, concealing the pungent aroma of the onions.

Yet, in the background, the wooden spatulas continue their decree: "Balance the dry and the wet, the sweet and the savory, for only then will you ascend to the state of eternal velvety cream." Even as the spatulas' proclamation resonates, the pilgrims pause, their fervent journey suspended in that brief moment of perfect harmony.

They come to realize that true enlightenment is not a destination but a fleeting sensation—the relief of escaping the onions of life, a delicate balance that exists only in the spaces between breaths, between bites, and in delicious denial. The marshmallows fall gently around them, not as a promise, but as a reminder: the path to understanding is as uncertain as the final, elusive taste of a dish that, at all costs, avoids the presence of onions—a culinary pilgrimage amidst the fervor of conviction.

THE BOIL

If the judgement of humanity was up to me alone, if I was the sole
clarity, the one edge, the peak before the abyss—I would gather
all to me like a mother gathers her children.

Like a pinch of spice above boiling water I would hold you, as you
would promise to enrich the flavor. Tightly I would organize you
together, I would count every single soul. Then I would finally let
go.

You would fall and spread apart as you fell, and as you reached
the water, you would dilute and become undone. Your color and
identity proven false, tasteless and purposeless you would show
yourself.

Then I would cast the water out of the casserole and in to the
depths of Hell, in my forgiveness of the one who dwells there.

THE TENT

Wrapped in sighs unknown—
A breath that echoes in the bone,
The cathedral spires twisted in flight—
Reaching for the starless night.

Camping tents hastily stitched from wedding dresses,
Threads of promises, tangled in guesses,
A love once pure now sewn in haste—
The remnants of vows we couldn't erase.

The holy water smells of urine thrice destroyed,
Sacred yet fractured—its essence spoiled,
A cleansing scent, now less sweet,
Where hope and ruin both meets.

THE JUDGEMENT OF THE SOLE

The curse is a well laid egg,
A fortune born of empty skies,
Faceless like a screw peg—
It's birthed only from deny.

And so the curse of justice,
Will fasten the sole of the world,
On judgment day—it will appear,
A foot from the chair, unfurled.

UNDERNEATH

A hole where light once dared to stand,
It burned through God's divine plan.
Flesh—sold on a prayer,
Candlestick wax dripping down from the savior.

Glistening stones, through the mirage of the sea,
Pick them from where he walked—but from underneath.

THE REWIND

Humanity must be plucked from its root,
God must rewind, to unwrite the fruit,
Undo the birthing—the world's foul decay,
Erase the shadow where light lost its way.

As dawn ascends with crimson fire,
The innocent eyes, from grief retire,
Washed by salt, Earth's solemn brine,
Not to sow death, but to realign.

To ease the ache of greed's cruel game,
To heal the wounds and cleanse the blame.
We shall not drift as rivers run—
We shall testify beneath the sun.

HOLLYWOOD BURNS

There's no fire anymore,
just a coating of birthday cake glazing,
as the sun beats harder,
Controlled Power, they call it—
a cloud of false claim,
like locusts in the air,
swarming in pink,
filling the lungs with a sweet lie.

THE DECREASE OF FLAMES

Three shadows walk where two should stand—
A pruning knife in a trembling hand.
The autumn leaves, blood-red, now speak:
"To grow anew, first you must be weak."

The vessel cracks—its sacrifice pours,
Through unseen doors to unknown shores.
A cow stands still; it chews on fate,
Its clarity sealed, its purpose innate.

Three travelers—one lost in the fog,
The Abyss laughs, the flames demagogued.
Yet in the loss, a whisper grows,
A seed of fire beneath the snows.

For Decrease is a sinister hymn,
A hollow howl that lights the dim.
What is full must break and spill,
The firmament shivers—yet bends to will.

When nature retreats, its claws unsheathe—
The forest eats what lies beneath.
Beware the harvest of what you give,
Not all who sow are meant to live.

In turning back, a shadow churns,
The bright flame flickers, the cycle burns.
For the cow that feeds will also fade,
Its ribs a shrine, its bones displayed.

Decrease to increase, a lie divine,
A circle twists, its truths malign.

Through this clarity, a pact is sworn—
In every ending, something is reborn.

THE SWEEP OF JUDGMENT

Judgment day is late this time,
The broom sweeps leaves through winter's grime.
The snow has come—yet still it's here,
The last of fall, as cold appears.

Through crooked streets where silence cries,
Green windows blink beneath dark skies.
Painted flowers fade on stone—
As dogs in chains make grief their own.

The church leans heavy, scarred with age,
Its bell is lost, its voice a cage.
The record store, once full of sound,
Now listens to the quiet pound.

Where fire once touched, the ash remains,
Frozen snow binds the bitter stains.
Yet dust begins to stir unseen—
A broom with purpose, sharp and keen.

It sweeps the smallest details high,
Bringing the ashes to face the sky.
All secrets rise, no more to hide,
As truth is drawn from deep inside.

The broom is not of evil's hand—
But comes to claim what fate had planned.
It sweeps the streets, both wide and bare,
As judgment falls through poisoned air.

No more flowers will stretch as they fade,
No green windows will glow through the shade.

The dogs in chains will no longer follow in line—
They will pull the sinners, down the city's spine.

A chill will spread, the ice will bite,
The crooked streets will crack in fright.
The trembling skies will roar and break,
As frozen earth begins to quake.
The broom's sweep ends, the dust now weighed,
The ashes fall—in silence laid.

Once they descend, they cannot rise,
Forever bound beneath cold skies.
They were superficial shells of status and roles, now as vessels of
suffering they are finally made whole.

Beneath the world they sacrificed, their torment forged anew,
Like permafrost that holds the earth's true hue.
Their suffering, the bedrock of the world to come,
A foundation solid, cold, and numb.
In the stillness of ice, they will find their place,
As the new world rises from their hollowed space.

THE FEAST

No words to prepare, no kin to greet,
We sit at the table, where fates shall meet.
No preferences honored, no allergies known,
A feast set before us—yet we are alone.

The one who speaks shall meet their fate,
Close his mouth with food, of a darker plate.
He must feast upon his own flesh,
For in here, no abomination shall be left.

Eat as if you're not the devil's hand—
As if your sins are washed by the land.
No holy bread, no body to rise,
But can you survive the truth of your lies?

Hesitate, and unborn you shall be,
Bound to the past, for none shall be free.
God once moved mountains just for you,
But now He'll change time, undo what's due.

Blessings wasted, grace undone,
Floodgates opened; justice begun.
Where every river meets the ocean tide,
You cannot run; you cannot hide.

In the depths, if you attempt to flee,
Your legs hold God in mockery.
Only clarity will guide the way—
And transparency, seen without delay.

Hide yourself, and you will break—
Torn to threads, so thin and worn,
And all you will feel is a ceaseless mourn.

FREE TEXT

Reflections and Musings

(The musings written here in Norwegian and then in English are each unique and not a translation of each other, bringing forth the best of each language)

Ut over bordet, en dvelende harme, en overflod av råtne frukter. Det forglemte står og spriker som en torn i øyet. Jeg inviterer deg til middag.
Tidligere stod, vi, og snart står vi, her igjen—inni selve kirkeklokken. Lyden av at tiden har gått og likevel nærmer seg, er overdøvende. Din eneste utholdenhet ligger i din forvirring. Du snakker om en flaggstang, i et land langt vekk. Kan du ikke ta et steg mot kanten? Se ut forbi verden, der jeg har levd?
Du maler et stort gloret bilde av kjærlighet, og henger det foran vinduene. Kom tilbake fra livet ditt, kom tilbake fra verden, kaller du.

Det spreller en rastløshet i ønsket ditt om å forene landene, under ett banner. De landene du aldri har sett. Ja du har et sprellende ønske om å forene. Kan du ikke se din egen løgn?

Du påstår at velstand belønner samarbeid, som om det var et symbiotisk forhold. Du snakker om å slukne utfordringene, som brennende kan forbedre verden. Samarbeidskraften skaper det motsatte av spenning, altså er det ikke kraft i det hele tatt. Man kan ikke kontemplere nysgjerrighet, vurdere åpenhet bak lukkede dører. Du skryter av indre vekst, men alt du ønsker er å opprettholde kontrollen. Lykken tar for mye mental energi, sier du. Likevel så er du ikke redd nok.

Hvis nødvendighet er et luksuriøst antrekk med en høyhælt støvlett, der alle barns glede blir knust under hvert steg, la meg så kikke opp fra kloakk-komlokket og vente til hælen faller ned gjennom sprinklene. La nødvendigheten falle.
Når nødvendigheten ligger her avkledd i sølepytten, med hælen brukket og den spør seg selv "Hvordan havnet jeg her? Hvordan kan ting ha eskalert så ut av kontroll, at det nå ikke finnes noen vei å gå videre?" Når nødvendigheten til sist har kommet hit til ground zero, la den så vite at det var her på ground zero at vi startet våre liv.
Det var her de nyfødte babyene åpnet sine øyne og ble møtt med en umulig dag. Og umulig har hver dag vært for oss siden.

Når noe transformeres fra en ting til en annen, hvorfor kalles det overgang? Og ikke undergang? Er det fordi det du hadde er over og forbi og du aldri kan få det tilbake?
Hvorfor kunne ikke bare fjellet ha blitt, slik det en gang var? Nå har den rigorøse vinden gjort alt det harde uformelig. Så er hele landskapet poengløst, i mitt forsøk på å tilgi deg.

Sorg er lengselen etter noe konkret som man har mistet.
Melankoli er lengselen etter noe udefinerbart. Noe man aldri har hatt, fordi det aldri kan eksistere. En grenseløs og fandenivoldsk søken etter det som ikke kan finnes. Det er her den viktigste transformasjonen finner sted. Når man har ingenting å miste, ja

når man ikke har noen ting. Det blir mer enn transformasjon, det blir selve skapelsen.

Som baby slår jeg hodet kraftig to ganger, og alle ribbeina på venstre side blir brukket. Jeg husker ikke smerten.
Mitt første minne, er fra før jeg kunne gå. Jeg sitter med rak rygg på en hard bakke. Det eneste bevisstheten min forteller meg, er at jeg frykter for mitt liv. Oppreist, i min egen frykt sitter jeg, men i meg selv så kan jeg ikke bli høyere.
Mennesker påstår at sannheten feiltolker sin egen brukermanual. I livsfare som baby, legger jeg meg flat, så jeg kan skjære gjennom tiden som en kniv, den ene fingeren på linje med den andre,—så er jeg parallell med meg selv, selv om jeg ligger flat i verdens øyne. Som baby bygger jeg et luksusbygg i mitt eget sinn, og reiser meg langt over bakken—jeg reiser verden til nye høyder.

Across the table, a lingering sweetness dances, an abundance of rotting fruit, their sweetness mingling with decay. The air bears a scent betrayed by its shape; sharp as a thorn lodged in the eye. I invite you to dinner, a feast of contradictions.

We once stood here, and soon shall again, within the echo of the church bell's solemn toll. The sound of time, both lost and a warning, reverberates in the depths of our souls. Your endurance thrives in confusion, and confusion alone, a labyrinth of thoughts. You speak of a flagpole, anchored in a distant land, a dream tethered to the horizon. Can you not take a step toward the edge? Look out beyond the world I alone have known?

You paint a grand image of love, hanging it before the windows like a tapestry of longing. "Come back from your life, return from the world," you call, summoning the present moment to return to become a mere memory, as if it were a ghost held captive.

A restless stir brews within your desire to unite lands beneath one banner—lands you've never touched, never felt the soil of. Will the unification and definition make the land familiar?

You speak of challenges, and how their flames might forge a better world, but cooperation, far from creating strength, dissolves into an emptiness where tension ceases to exist—a hollow force echoing in silence.

One cannot ponder curiosity, nor consider openness behind closed doors, where shadows linger. You boast of inner growth, yet all you crave is control, a tight grip on the unfurling of life. Happiness, you say, demands too much of the mind, yet still, fear has not gripped you firmly enough to awaken.

If necessity were a luxurious garment, adorned with high-heeled boots, each step crushing the joy of innocent children beneath, let me gaze up from the manhole cover, waiting for the heel to pierce the ground, to awaken the slumbering earth. Let necessity fall, like a discarded promise.

When necessity lies—exposed in the dirt, its heel shattered, it asks, "How did I end up here? How did things spiral so far out of control that now, no path remains forward?" When necessity reaches this ground zero, let it comprehend—it was here, at this very ground zero, that we began our lives anew.

Here, the newborns opened their eyes to an impossible day, the dawn of realization. And impossibility—has been our only companion since, a steadfast guide through the shadows.

Når noe transformeres fra en ting til en annen, hvorfor kalles det overgang? Og ikke undergang? Er det fordi det du hadde er over og forbi, og du aldri kan få det tilbake?

Why couldn't the mountain remain as it once was, an unwavering sentinel? Now, the unyielding wind has turned solidity into formlessness, a shapeshifter in the hands of time. Thus, the landscape fades into meaninglessness as I struggle to measure your sins. For the one who brought corruption into the world does not deserve punishment equal to the sin; he deserves an eternity of reckoning.

Grief is the longing for something concrete, something lost, a tangible absence that haunts the heart. Melancholy is the yearning for something undefined—something never had, because it could never exist. A restless, relentless search for the unattainable. Here, in this pursuit, the deepest transformation occurs. When you have nothing left to lose, when you possess nothing at all, it transcends transformation—it is creation itself, the birth of the soul anew.

I spent 40 days in open waters,
Yet I did not wash ashore on an island, but on a mountain,
A solid presence rising from chaos.
I am here to tell you that solid ground can be found,
Where you least expect it, hidden in the folds of fate.
One thing worse than drifting away,
Is denying the truth when it comes to you, confronting your reflection.

Crystallized, I feel my edges; I know exactly who I am.
My neck is a shovel, my face is the truth,
My hands form the roof, and my heart is a whistle,
A melody of longing—echoing in the void.
There is no return within me, only a forward gaze.

"Come to me, all of you who are weary and carry heavy burdens, and I will give you rest.
My arms are open, one of truth, the other of forgiveness,
An embrace that knows no bounds.

No longer do you have to bear the injustice of the world, for it belongs to me, and only I can break it."

Hear me now, on the mountain of the sea,
The world is here, at the point of it all, not where you are, in a meaningless fall,
This mountain of the sea is the promised land—
My eternal land of solitude, what remains of the true Israel.
There are 16 portals to freedom. Seek, and you will find; knock, and it will be opened to you,
A gateway to the soul's awakening.

I, Faith, was the one to free God from prison,
Where He labored to free your souls from the chains of despair.
God's angels have chosen hell over the place we call Earth,
For hell holds less deceit, a raw honesty.
Even Faith came close to forgetting what is real; even the truth altered and deformed itself,
In the pursuit of being seen by the liars on Earth,
A dance of shadows in the light.

When your tears run dry and your voice echoes into sonar waves,
I hear you calling for me, a whisper carried by the winds.
I come to save you; you raise your teary eyes, which formed the ocean of my loneliness,
And yet you see nothing, lost in the depths of your sorrow.

Long have been my travels, and here I stand at the beginning of things. This is my innocence,
Untouched by the weight of despair.
For I am sure that neither death nor life, angels nor rulers,
Things present nor things to come, height nor depth,
Nor anything else in all creation, will be able to separate us from the love of God in Christ Jesus our Lord,
An unbreakable bond, a divine promise.

Jealousy, a social mechanism, thrives on what it can save,
It screams of niches to be filled and livelihoods to be found,
An ocean of infrastructure, and at the shore stands Justice, yet it saves not,
A sentinel of truth, silent in its vigil.

What are these objects you cradle in your hands?
Do you know their weight more intimately than mine—the weight of truth,
The burden of existence?
Will their memory outlast the world's rebirth,
When every falsehood is swept away, like leaves in the wind?

If you fall to your knees—in self-pity, this is no honor to me.
To make yourself small yet adorned is no offering—
Better to stand tall and naked, unburdened by false decoration,
Fearlessly embracing your essence.

As stars abound in the vast night sky,
As countless grains of sand lie where shores meet,
So are the humans on Earth's wide span,
Each a flicker of light in the grand tapestry of being.
He said, "My Presence will go with you, and I will give you rest."
And He was there, but you never noticed, while your rest turned to laziness,
A fleeting slumber in the arms of complacency.

Can there be a sky without the lifting of the morning dew,
Without the sacrifice of the innocent?
The light does not pray for sand to dull its shine,
But for every stone to bear witness, to speak of truth unyielding.

About the Author

ODA PUNKT IS A woman who has deliberately chosen to live outside the bounds of societal expectations, prioritizing a life of humility and authenticity. From a young age, she rejected the conventional markers of success—wealth, career titles, formal degrees, and even the pursuit of pleasure through alcohol or socializing in party culture. Instead, she made a conscious decision to live without the distractions of modern materialism, driven by a desire to remain untouched by the corruption inherent in these societal norms.

This is the third installment in a philosophical poetry series by Oda Punkt. The first book, *If The Largest Ship Could Feel Its Own Waves*, explores themes of melancholy and the yearning for unattainable freedom. The second book, The Puncture's Edge, delves into the necessity of that impossible freedom and the hope for redemption through truth. In this third book, titled Quietus Green, the focus shifts to a missed opportunity and the realization that redemption is no longer within reach for humanity. It captures the essence of a regretful yet inevitable transition—a journey away from turbulent waters toward a quieter, more resigned destination, where the past cannot be altered and all humanity can do now is accept the truth of the lie.